119

DC

60uC

Victorian and Edwardian

CHILDREN

from old photographs

A.J. and D.K. PIERCE

B.T. BATSFORD Ltd
LONDON

First published 1980
© A.J. and D.K. Pierce 1980

ISBN 0 7134 2327 7

Filmset in Monophoto Apollo by
Servis Filmsetting Ltd, Manchester

Printed in Great Britain by
Butler & Tanner Ltd, London and Frome
for the publishers, B.T. Batsford Ltd,
4 Fitzhardinge St, London W1H 0AH

CONTENTS

ACKNOWLEDGMENTS

The Authors and Publishers wish to thank the following organisations and individuals for allowing copies to be made from original photographs in their possession or for supplying prints:

Bradford Museums and Art Galleries: 20, 25, 27, 30, 32, 34, 38, 61, 69, 70, 111, 137.

Burnley Public Library: 47, 81–84, 93, 109, 112–116, 129.

Craven Museum, Skipton: 3, 18, 21, 22, 26, 28, 29, 40, 43, 59, 76, 96, 126.

Derbyshire Museum Service, Sudbury Hall, Museum: 5, 15, 39, 52, 54, 74, 89–91, 128.

I. Dewhirst: 31, 41, 86, 100, 119, 134.

Gentleman's Society, Spalding: 6, 11, 14, 16, 35, 53, 101, 117, 118, 124.

D.D. Gladwin: 94, 110.

N. Halstead: 33.

N. Higgin: 68.

D. Hollingshead: 17.

Keighley Public Library: 24, 65, 87, 88, 105, 106.

Leeds City Libraries: 9, 19, 23, 37, 42, 45, 49, 66, 71, 75, 99.

N. Livesley: 63, 85, 102.

W. Lord: 109.

Metropolitan Borough of Stockport Library of Social Studies: 95, 97, 98, 103, 104, 107.

Nelson Local History Society: 108.

N. Newbold: 10.

S. Payne: 8.

M. Peatson: 91.

St. Christopher's: 36, 48, 50, 51.

Shibden Hall Museum, Halifax: 4, 7, 46, 55, 58, 62, 67, 77, 79, 80, 120–122, 125, 127, 132, 135.

P. Stibbens: 130, 133, 136.

J. Thorpe: 73.

G. Turbutt: 72.

A. Van der Weyden: 2.

E. Williams: 1, 12, 57.

Wisbech and Fenland Museum: 13, 44, 64, 92, 123.

Other photographs not acknowledged above are from the Authors' collection.

In addition the Authors wish to thank numerous individuals for their patient help in researching this book, as well as Pennine Graphic Studios, H.S. Harrison, L. Smith and N.K. Howarth for photographic work, Mrs N. Hicken and Mrs C. Kirby for typing, Mr I. Dewhirst for carefully examining hundreds of photographs and Mr & Mrs D.D. Gladwin for constant encouragement.

INTRODUCTION

A VIEW OF LIFE

The period covered by the photographs in this book is from the start of Queen Victoria's reign until the beginning of the First World War, and was one of great change in the lives of children in Britain.

Undoubtedly over both Victoria and Edward's reign the lot of children in general improved; Factory Acts, ensuring that child labour became less widespread, and Education Acts at last giving Government backing to the work that voluntary organisations had been doing for many years previously. Looked at more specifically, a great divide still existed between children of the wealthier classes and those from the working classes. Similarly, the ways of life of children of these two groups varied considerably and to a great extent this is reflected in the photographs shown in this book. For children of the poorer areas of inner cities their inclusion in photographs was a result usually of either their being used for scale purposes or from their natural curiosity. As is apparent from the photographs, whichever purpose the children were photographed for, their environmental conditions are all too clear. Happily, on a number of the photographs, a child's natural sense of humour comes through even in the most harrowing circumstances.

As at all times the selection of photographs is limited by what the Victorian and Edwardian photographers chose to take. Much of Victorian children's history seems to revolve around the hardships endured by many thousands of children in the mills, factories and mines of the Industrial Revolution. Few people can be without an image of the child sweeps, match girls, or of the ragged child looking, bewildered, at the camera. Certainly children such as these existed, and in large numbers. Great numbers of unwanted children were thrown upon the mercy of workhouses and ruthless factory masters. In 1837, the year of Victoria's accession, nearly 40,000 unwanted children are estimated to have been born. No problem is new!

It is also true that the plight of these children was rarely one to be recorded by the camera, perhaps reflecting some conscience on the part of people in the system; or, more likely, the cumbersome equipment of early photographers precluded such photographs. An overriding reason, of course, is that little purpose existed in photographing children at work; it was far too mundane an aspect of everyday life to be recorded by the new and rapidly growing technique of photography.

Nevertheless, children have always formed an essential part of people's curiosity; the picture of a baby has always evoked suitable comments from doting grandparents or casual visitors (to say nothing of Politicians) confronted with a photograph. The popularity of the 'carte de visite' in the later Victorian period provided photographers with an opportunity which they still prize today of taking photographs of babies and young children. It was, of course, mainly the babies of better off families whose photographs we are now able to examine. Nevertheless, this is a fascinating exercise; not only the clothing of the children but also their facial expressions provide much of great interest and amusement. It is obvious that many parents and grandparents went to great pains to ensure the correct 'costume' was worn for the photographic occasion. Naturally the most intriguing feature of this is identifying the boys from the girls at an early age when it was customary to dress the boys very much in the style of girls until they were breeched at the age of 4 or 5 years. Even then, as is clear in some of the photographs, some boys faced the camera with great indignity.

As the lives of children in general changed dramatically during the period, the change is reflected in the photographs of the children. From about the turn of the century, with dry plate processes giving a greater freedom to the photographer, the photographs became less posed and we are able to see children in more natural surroundings.

CLOTHES AND FASHION

In order to gain background to the photographs in this book I feel it is necessary to look briefly at the main aspects of children's lives during the period.

Fashion, as today, changed frequently, for children fortunate enough to be properly clothed. One of the few fashions approved of by boys was the sailor suit, which appears on many photographs posed and unposed. All too often, as in the case of the Fauntleroy suit, popular in the 1880s, the wearer of the clothes felt distinctly uncomfortable. Noticeably, some fashions were designed as a miniaturised version of a man's suit, the tweed material Norfolk suit being an example of this.

In the 1840s girls' pantalettes, or knickers, were clearly visible and are so in several photographs, while the wide crinoline forced on many girls must have caused problems moving about in the nursery. For the overwhelming majority, however, clothes were at least secondhand and fashion did not enter into it.

AT PLAY

Most children of the middle and upper classes spent much of their playtime in the nursery, which was often stocked with a delightful selection of toys, beautifully crafted. The growth in popularity of the railways resulted in model railways becoming the 'toy of the moment'. Fortunately for us photographs remain showing beautifully made replicas of the railway system. The favourite toy undoubtedly was the nursery rocking horse made sturdily of wood and brightly painted, more expensive models even sporting a mane of real horse hair.

The dolls house too was a great favourite with girls and often these were intricately made down to minute details, possibly as part of a girls training for later life. Tin or lead soldiers were collected by many boys who re-created famous battles.

For large numbers of children the street rather than the nursery was their playground and toys such as those described above were viewed only in toy shop windows.

During Victoria's reign many beautiful dolls were made and, almost universally among girls, the doll was perhaps the favourite toy. Even some of the poorest children can be seen proudly clutching a doll, perhaps made simply of a wooden spoon and rag, but nevertheless having a common link with their wealthier counterparts. The faces of wax and china dolls, many of which have survived today, are a near perfect replica of the human face, and walking and talking dolls reflected the spirit of inventiveness which pervaded life in Victoria's reign.

For older children the toy theatre, with its hair-raisingly dangerous row of oil-burning wicks as footlights, became a way of spending many hours. Children from a great variety of walks of life could join in this entertainment, buying the penny plain or tuppence coloured characters and scenery to enliven their theatre.

No doubt stirred by theatre posters and adult tales, charades and play making became a widespread pastime, particularly in Edwardian times when, largely due to Edward VII himself, theatre-going became a great entertainment.

Samplers, pieces of embroidery skilfully made by girls, showed intricate landscapes or letters of the alphabet and many hours were spent on this occupation, the final result often becoming a birthday card or present.

For the vast majority of children, however, it was outdoor games that took up their free time. In the cities the street was the playground; country children, though perhaps being no wealthier financially, had a healthier environment in which to play. In the country, particularly, outdoor games changed according to the season as, to an extent, they do today. Hoop rolling – either an iron or wooden one – and marbles, were popular pastimes and football, played for centuries, increased in popularity, the foundation of todays football league teams being laid in Victoria's reign. For many children life was far from dull, even if entertainment meant hanging around the gas-lit street corners or sitting on the kerb, mischief-making at the slightest opportunity.

The Victorian and Edwardian cameraman gave us a glimpse of these activities from which we can see the stark contrast of the beautiful dolls, dolls houses and tin trains, to the street life.

HOLIDAYS

In 1871 Bank Holidays were established in this country enabling all people, theoretically, to enjoy an official holiday. For generations people had enjoyed time honoured occasions, kept perhaps more in the country than in towns. May Day and the end of harvest gave respite from work but for the multitudes, including children who had gone willingly or unwillingly to provide labour for Britain's new Industrial Wealth, the Bank Holiday provided the first real chance for a holiday, although a day's pay would be lost. Coupled with this, the development of the railways had brought places previously inaccessible within reach of masses of people.

The canals too, forerunners of the railways, provided day trips, and waggonettes or charabancs drawn by patient horses opened up the countryside and seaside to ever increasing numbers. Sunday Schools provided many children with their first outing of this kind and a large number of pictures of these events survive to remind us not only of earlier forms of transport but also of happy days in what was for some a largely unhappy life.

Once at the seaside there were an ever increasing number of attractions to tempt young and old alike. Just as today, the beach was for children the greatest attraction, and many photographs show them engaged in pastimes continued today, digging in the sand or donkey riding.

Before finding popularity as a holiday resort some towns had existed as fishing villages. At these places, Cromer for example, the return home of the fishing fleet provided an opportunity for children to either simply watch, or else to stand by the boats in the hope of either receiving an offering from the catch or earning a few pence by helping with the unloading.

No seaside holiday was complete without the family photograph and from these we can see that holidays had become, by the end of our period, available to the majority of families even if only on a day trip.

The Pier proved a great attraction for all; the side shows, slot machines and, on many piers, a concert hall held children and adults alike enthralled – indeed the pier became the very symbol of a thriving resort.

The opening of public parks, either by councils or private benefactors, provided children with new open spaces in which to play. On any fine afternoon large collections of nannies could be found with their charges, sporting the latest in prams and no doubt comparing nursery notes.

ATTITUDES

It has been said that childhood barely existed for most British children at the end of the eighteenth century, as they began a lifetime of labour as soon as they could do very simple jobs. For the children of many middle and upper class families however, childhood certainly did exist, after a fashion. For these children perhaps the typical image of the aloof Victorian father with children who should be seen and not heard held true. Indeed many fathers seemed to feel the children should not be seen either. While the mother saw her children frequently, though generally in the nursery, father saw little of his children, almost the whole task of the upbringing of the children being left to the nurse or governess. In the Nursery, even one equipped with its wealth of toys, life was strictly regulated.

Towards the end of the century, however, a more enlightened attitude on the part of parents began to spread, resulting in far greater contact between parent and child.

For the children at the opposite end of the spectrum contact with parents was also restricted, though not for the same reasons.

Leaving early in the morning for work, maybe as piecers in a northern mill, the children returning home at night were too tired to have time for parents, and vice versa. As the century wore on and Royal Commissions exposed the scandals of child labour, the lessening of hours worked led to greater freedom for children. The introduction of the Education Acts, particularly in 1870 and 1876, meant of course that the child's time not spent at work was spent at school, or should have been.

Prior to these Acts the Commissioners' Reports on child labour conditions in mines and factories began to produce an increase in concern for the conditions of children, and gradually the lot of working children did improve, culminating in the Consolidation Act of 1878. By this Act no child under eight years was to be employed in any craft, children under twelve years could only work on a half time system and the maximum for children was twelve hours a day, with $1\frac{1}{2}$ hours for meal times and at least ten hours at school weekly.

Under the 1876 Education Act full time education for children up to ten years of age became compulsory. The problem with this, of course, was that the School Board officials had great difficulty in ensuring that children did attend. The last chapter in the Victorian child's story was written in 1891, when full time employment for children under eleven years was prohibited, so ending probably the greatest evil of Victorian life.

While our vision of child labour revolves round mines and factories we should not forget the country child. By the age of seven or eight boys had become bird scarers from early morning till dusk; weeding and stone picking were other occupations forced upon children. Whilst these children at least enjoyed the benefits of fresh air, other country children working in the domestic industry of small cottages were little better than their factory counterparts.

Harvest time, naturally, demanded the services of all children and indeed when, in 1876, the Government banned the employment of children under the age of ten, this excluded harvest time.

EDUCATION

As children spent less time at work this was parallelled by a rise in the demand for children to receive education. It must be said, however, that not all adults felt children should be prevented from working. Daniel Defoe on his great tour of England was delighted to see young children at work, as young even as four years.

The development of schooling culminating in the 1876 Education Act had begun many years previously, and while the great majority of early Victorian children had no schooling, the sons of wealthier parents often attended boarding schools. For others the Churches tried hard to provide some form of education, opening the National and British Schools, but almost invariably these comprised one large classroom with possibly up to one hundred children and only one teacher, whose job of educating became virtually impossible. Older pupils, the monitors, helped him and provided a basis of reading for the children who attended – a start at least was made.

Some of the less wealthy children attended Dame Schools, run usually by old ladies in their front parlour with few books, seats or desks, but nevertheless charging a weekly fee. Perhaps the greatest school attendances, however, were made at the Sunday Schools established at both Churches and Chapels. Sunday being a free day for almost everybody ensured a good attendance at these Schools, and following on the establishment of the first Sunday School in 1780 a rapid expansion had taken place. However, some children were considered too ragged to be allowed into any school and therefore stood no chance of learning anything. This led to the establishment of the 'ragged' schools – either Sunday or Day Schools which began in London and rapidly spread through the country – which in 1844 came together under the auspices of the Ragged School Union.

It is almost ironic that certain Mill Owners paraded their child apprentices each Sunday for Sunday School, ensuring, of course, that they were smartly dressed.

Although boarding schools existed their reputation often left much to be desired, a fact exposed in the writing of Charles Dickens. Nevertheless, by the middle of the nineteenth century, boarding schools had taken on a somewhat better image, largely due to Thomas Arnold, founder of Rugby School.

It was with the passing of the 1870 Education Act that changes really took place, and rather than somewhat despising education, people began to look up to it with some pride. Perhaps as a consequence of this, school activities became more photographed, different School Boards almost trying to outdo each other in the range of subjects offered. Fairly quickly there followed the establishment of schools for the disabled, until by the reign of Edward VII school and education had become expected and acceptable.

Many fine photographs exist of these new schools and the lessons taking place within them, and it makes an interesting task to compare them with modern day schools and lessons. One of the most interesting lessons to look at is P.T., or drill, where some of the clothing worn must have been most cumbersome.

Craft, sometimes thought of as a newcomer to the school curriculum today, was in good evidence. In many schools some of the detailed work produced was of a very high standard.

FAMILY LIFE

Having looked briefly at some aspects of children's lives let us look at family life, certainly the most important aspect of a child's world. More so during the Victorian era than the Edwardian, children could be divided into the haves and have nots.

For the middle classes, Victoria's long reign was happy and prosperous, the large families with ten or more children often being aided by servants. Such children referred to their fathers as 'Papa' or often 'Sir'. While father and, to a lesser extent, Mother, saw far less of their children than today's parents, they nevertheless regarded the children's upbringing as a great responsibility, with a firm belief in the teaching of right and wrong. For girls it was firmly held that, if they were to marry the 'right' type of boy, they should learn music, singing, dancing, drawing and deportment. Domestic tasks, it was considered, would never really concern them and consequently were of little importance. By the 1870s, however, this view had begun to change, girls and young women having begun to assert themselves more. As a fuel to this type of thinking, a number of boarding schools for girls opened in the 1850s, teaching so-called modern, previously unthinkable subjects such as cookery.

For the majority of Victorian children punishment was hard and instantaneous, the principle of 'Spare the rod and spoil the child' being firmly adhered to. Lies and disobedience were serious offences for children which warranted caning. Despite this, middle class children of the age generally regarded their childhood as a happy time. Most of them formed part of a closely knit family group which in many instances they did not leave for the whole of their lives. In this somewhat sheltered environment they had little contact with their contemporaries, the have nots. This is not to say that all middle class Victorian parents were ignorant of the problems of the poorer classes. Indeed, the founding of several societies to help the poorer child was a direct result of the concern of the middle classes.

The poorer children shared at least some aspects of middle class life. In many cases the closeness of family life was as great among them as it was in the middle and upper classes, although life itself with a shortage of money was certainly more difficult. Conditions of large families in small houses obviously meant overcrowding, with three or even more children to a bed, it not being unknown for children to sleep head to toe.

Certainly the worst off children were those of the very low paid families, where a great fear of the workhouse with all its evils pervaded family life. Thousands were forced to the workhouses through no fault of their own. Once in the workhouse, the family was invariably split up and the children suffered the indignities, not only of separation from their parents, but also of a close-cropped haircut and workhouse clothing. Under such circumstances, it is little wonder that these children grew up with a great feeling of resentment of all they knew. For most parents a great fear, perhaps comparable with that of the workhouse, was the death of a young child. Infant mortality ran at a high rate even among wealthy families, but among the poorer classes, living in cramped, unsanitary conditions, the risk was increased manyfold. Children died of diseases often spread by foul drinking water, open sewers, rotting rubbish in the streets, lack of proper toilet or washing facilities and from polluted air, particularly in factory towns. Living closely together in these conditions, children had little natural immunity to such diseases as scarlet fever, measles, polio or tuberculosis. Once one member of a family contracted such a disease there was a serious risk of it rapidly spreading among the other children. Lack of good food and damp cold houses led, if not to death, to rickets and other crippling diseases. This in itself led to the establishment of homes for the disabled.

EDWARDIAN CHANGES

By the turn of the century, with the flamboyance of Edwardian England spreading throughout all levels of society, conditions began to improve. School medical inspections began in 1907 and slum clearance programmes paved the way for progress which is continuing even today. Also in 1907 the first Boy Scout Group gave boys an opportunity of belonging to a group whose activities considerably widened their horizons. Firm foundations had been laid in this direction by the founding of the Boys Brigade in 1883.

The foundation of the N.S.P.C.C. in 1884 led to a greater public and parental awareness of the physical cruelty to which some children were being exposed and served to prick the nation's conscience. Nevertheless, as the new century dawned one third of British families still lived below the poverty line, and certain areas of our cities still suffered from high infant mortality despite a falling mortality rate overall.

The Education Service, whilst expanding, was complaining that many children were too ill-fed to learn successfully, and so free school meals were introduced in a number of areas, though not all Authorities took up the Government grants to enable them to provide the meals service.

In other areas too the Edwardian child was feeling the winds of change. The harsh Victorian punishments were gradually being replaced by a more humane attitude, which some would argue has continued and now gone too far.

Before 1900 Probation had been introduced for first offenders and in 1902 the first house for young offenders opened near a village which was to give its name to such Institutions even today, the village of Borstal. Juvenile Courts were established for all under 16 years of age and imprisonment of children under 14 was abolished totally. Certainly great steps had been taken in fifty years.

The Education Acts which saved children from full-time work could not prevent children, particularly of those who needed extra money to live, from working outside school hours as knockers up, errand boys, or lather boys in barbers shops. For some this must have been light relief from a somewhat dull school life, for though a wide and varied curriculum may have been provided its teaching may not have done it justice.

For wealthier parents and children the early part of the new century was a wonderful time with a wide range of mechanical, electric, and clockwork toys becoming available.

REFLECTIONS

Reflecting on the period as a whole and looking at the photographs of children taken during it, one is bound to draw analogies with children's lives today. Certainly some things have changed; the spending power of children today would be beyond the belief of their Victorian counterpart. Similarly the tremendous range of sweets, toys, books, comics and numerous other items would astound these children. Educational facilities too have developed beyond the wildest dreams of children who sat in high ceilinged classrooms. This is not to totally decry the efforts of our early education system, for great achievements were made.

Costume, which played so great a part in many children's lives, has altered in range and choice too, but just as the sailor suit became almost a uniform, so have the jeans and tee-shirt of today.

Despite the obvious differences in children of the two eras there are marked similarities.

Games and pastimes today would undoubtedly be recognised by children of Victorian times. Seasonally the same games come and go and, essentially, dolls today do no more or less than Victorian dolls. Indeed the dolls of the earlier period are possibly even more intricately designed and operated.

Special occasions bear great similarity. When we compare the photographs of Edward VII's Coronation celebrations with those of Queen Elizabeth II's Silver Jubilee, we still see the flag-waving children lining the streets awaiting the carnival procession or glimpse of the Royal Visitor. Where village carnivals or fetes are held, children form as much a centrepiece today as they did before.

Christmas, a time so enriched by Prince Albert, remains today, despite commercialisation, essentially a children's time.

Upon looking at many hundreds of photographs of children in preparing this book, one is time and again struck by the cheerfulness and natural curiosity of children — indeed the poorer the child the more cheerful he often appears to be. The posed photographs, predominantly from middle or upper class parents, often seem in some way to stifle the child's natural photogenic quality.

Perhaps the greatest satisfaction in examining the photographs of children in this period was the intense appeal child photographs have today, and obviously had in Victorian and Edwardian times. Most upper and middle class families made an effort to have at least the yearly photograph taken of their children, and a large number of them had several taken. Once holidays became popular it became almost obligatory for the holiday snapshot to be taken, sometimes in a posed situation looking remote from the seaside, or with at least a seaside background.

In other photographs the stiff-lipped determination of the Victorian father shows through, perhaps resisting the temptation to smile proudly at his children. The children too have often been told that they should not smile though the costumes they were forced into were sufficient to stop anyone smiling. Hairstyles, particularly of boys, were often produced specifically for the photographs; the ridicule any child would have suffered in the streets would have been beyond belief.

Similarly, the poses adopted in some photographs are so unreal as to give the picture an extra value, while others are so authentic that we develop a real feeling for the child in the photograph.

Note on the photographs

What we have attempted to do in this book is to show a selection of photographs which will reflect not a particular way of life in this changing period for children, but many ways of life. The photographs have been selected from many sources, mainly from unknown local photographers. The great majority of these photographs have never been published before; indeed, some of them were a revelation to their owners, that in fact they had them at all.

Similarly we have tried to cover a wide geographical range in the photographs, although we realised more and more that no matter where the photographs came from there was little overall difference in children. We have tried also to show a cross-section of children from different social classes; if there is an imbalance in favour of or against one type of child, this is purely accidental.

Our overriding aim in assembling this collection has been to portray the children as the camera saw them, sometimes posed, sometimes in a near natural situation. We have tried to show joy and sadness, very young children and very old children, special occasions and ordinary occasions.

We could have produced a book of photographs showing what is perhaps regarded as the typical photographs of children of the time. We chose not to do this, but rather to present a collection which we hoped would show a more ordinary, realistic image.

It is probably true to say that, just as today, there was no average child in Victorian and Edwardian times. Children were indeed very different, though they could be grouped by the area they lived in, their parents' occupations and various other categories. Some of this classification must naturally show through in our choice of photographs. What we particularly hope shows through is that children in the period covered were as individual as they always had been and always will be, that they were and are, simply children.

1 When they were very young

1   As at all times, beautifully dressed babies are appealing, and virtually indistinguishable one from another.

2 An Edwardian family group from Ewell, Surrey in 1910. The boy is wearing a velvet suit with a crocheted collar, a fashionable accessory of the period.

3 Whether with father or mother many babies found comfort in a dummy. In 1890 they were no doubt as frowned upon and loved as they are today.

4   An afternoon in the park was the ideal way for nannies to spend time with their nursery charges. This scene of about 1902 also shows older children under the charge of governesses.

5 An essential part of a baby's equipment even in Victorian times was the high chair. Even with the cushion the iron chair looks remarkably uncomfortable.

6 The photographers' favourite subjects, animals and babies. Lincolnshire, *c.*1890.

7 During Edward VII's reign the posed photograph became an essential part of every aspiring middle class household. The settings for such photographs were many and varied as too was the quality. The baby is oblivious to the occasion, the young boy bored and the mother proudly dressed in her best clothes. To whom the knees and boots on the left hand side belong we do not know.

8 A photograph of Mildred and Basil Bowyer taken in Messrs Wright's Studios, Forest Gate, London in 1893. The delightful wicker work carriage has a double hood for protection in wet weather, and a safety strap for the child at the front.

9 Despite his now distressing conditions this child was probably as beautiful a baby as the two in the previous photograph.

10   Phyllis born August 1897, Margaret born November 1898 and in the middle Norman born September 1900. The children of a Derbyshire farming family.

11   This little girl is proudly holding her doll, then, as now, the doll was a favourite toy of all girls. Many dolls made during this period reflected a great inventiveness.

12 When this photograph was taken in 1872 it was easier for the subject to visit the photographer where wondrous backgrounds could be created however incongruous they may now seem. Judging by their expressions these two children were reluctant subjects.

13 Some costumes of the period were obviously not appreciated by their wearers.

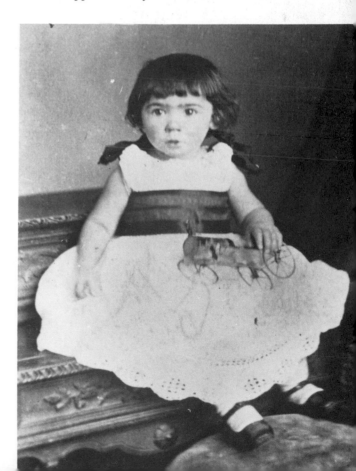

14 Even girls were given toys symbolising the age of the mobile steam engine. Christmas 1905 in Wallingford, Berkshire.

15 During the Edwardian period (this was taken in 1914) the doll continued to be a favourite toy of child and photographer alike.

16 For those who could afford a nursery, beautiful toys like this were available and could be seen in many toy shows in the 1870s. The best nurseries had to have a good selection of course.

2 At school

15　For those who could afford a nursery,

17　A Girls School group photographed in or near Hexham taken late in the last century. The photograph shows some uniformity of dress among the girls. The laced up boots worn by the girls on the front row are typical of ladies footwear of this period.

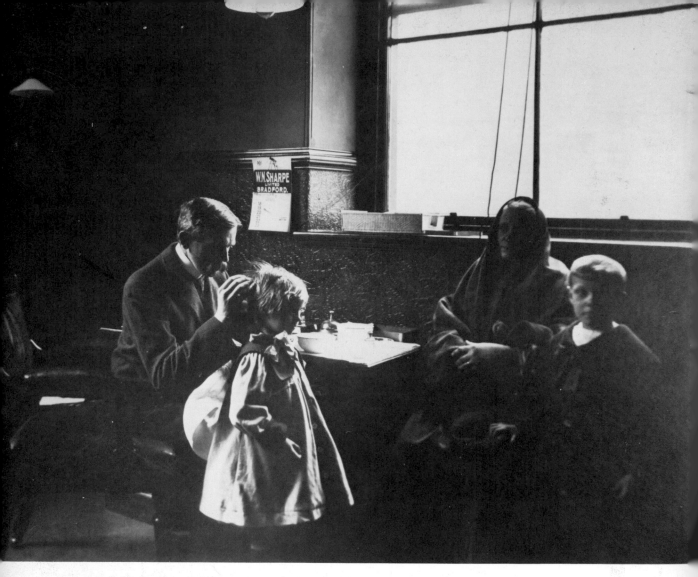

18 The elimination of disease among children became an important part of the new Board Schools. Children were regularly inspected for head lice, weighed and measured. Bradford, *c.*1907.

19 High-ceilinged classrooms were soon seen to have great potential for displaying children's work. This photograph is one of a collection from the Leeds School Board, 1901.

20 Cookery classes became part of many girls' education as this was seen as part of a training for running a future home. Photographs such as this show how much thinking on girls education has changed. Bradford, *c*.1907.

21 The growth and development of children in schools became a concern of the nation in the early part of this century. In 1907 medical inspection in school became compulsory.

22 Open air schools, particularly for handicapped children, were developed in some areas of the country at the turn of the century. The conditions in which the children learned were less crowded.

23 Special educational provision for blind children in Leeds. A geography lesson in progress during 1901.

24 'Unruly School Boys'. The boys in this clearly posed photograph were pupils at the Keighley Trade and Grammar School, about 1892. How closely the drawing of Thomas on the date board resembled the teacher's real face is unknown.

25 Even in 1879 fashion was important enough to be worn like a uniform.

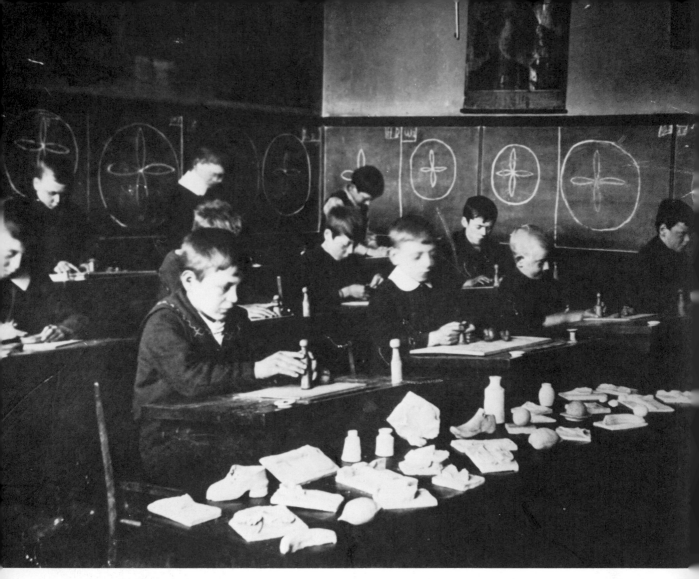

26 Considerable skill must have been necessary to produce some of these pottery objects.

27 Early school meals were prepared in what to the modern eye appears to be rather unsavoury conditions. Notice the bandage on the man's finger. Bradford, *c*.1907.

28 In 1907 the Government empowered local authorities to provide school meals as part of the new awareness of the poor physical condition of many children now compulsorily attending school. The girl on the front left appears to be out of favour.

29 School swimming instruction became part of the curriculum of many schools early this century. Here the boys, or their teachers, have developed a highly successful way of drying backs. The physical condition of some of the children is, unfortunately, all too obvious. Bradford in 1907.

30   A noticeable contrast in styles of swimming costume though the two
photographs were taken about the same time. Though an obviously posed photograph
this one certainly is a pose with a difference. Notice also the gas lighting.

31   'At Drill' was the title of this photograph, taken at Stanbury School, Yorkshire in
1902 by James Bradley, the school master of the time. He later achieved some fame in
pioneering nature study in schools using his own school as a model.

32 An early school photograph taken in the 1860s before compulsory education. Certainly these Yorkshire children were not those of the wealthy.

33 A group of schoolchildren in 1912. These children, however, were the pride of St John's School, Nelson, Lancashire for they had not been late or 'off school' for a whole year. We are told the teacher's name was Mr Hornby.

34 Basket making, a craft long established in the school curriculum, is here demonstrated by a class of mentally handicapped children. Bradford was notable in its attempts to provide an education for all types of children. One of two city fathers, W.E. Forster, being in the forefront of the move to educate children.

35 A Lincolnshire Grammar School October 1877. Notice the Mortar boards and gowns.

36 In the early Victorian period a girl's formal education did not include laundry work. By the outbreak of the First World War things had changed.

37 In some schools 'drill' was replaced by new and sophisticated P.E. equipment –
though the clothing does not appear very suitable for its use.

38 Schools without sophisticated P.E. equipment did 'drill' in the classroom. Note the aspidistra on the piano.

39 Drill formed an essential part of any Board School curriculum. In this 1870s photograph the 'P.E. Kit' must have been very uncomfortable.

40 Some early classrooms in the new Board Schools were less inspiring than others, though from the work on the board sounds and handwriting were taught. A not inelegant script by the teacher.

3 Daily life of the family

41 'Shovelling Snow'. A delightful caption given by the photographer Amos
Dewhirst to this group of children at the back of his tobacconist and newsagent shop
in Keighley, Yorks in 1905. Amos Dewhirst was a keen local photographer.

42 Children were pawns in many games, here they may have been used by the
photographer to give an added effect to the squalid surroundings.

43 The acquisition of a first suit complete with watch and chain was a proud occasion for many boys. *c.*1910.

45 Handcarts were used for a variety of purposes and children could earn a few pence wheeling them for different traders. Certainly these boys look sturdy and well fed for their work.

44 The machine having acquired pneumatic tyres, bicycle riding in the flat fen country became an ideal pastime for a well-to-do young lady.

46 Not a 'bull in a china shop' but three growing children. In this period children who would have the opportunity of later working in their fathers business were more fortunate than many of their contemporaries. The father here seems justifiably proud of his business.

47 Not only at the seaside were children and donkeys attracted to each other. This pre-1900 photograph shows someone's ingenuity with two bicycle wheels.

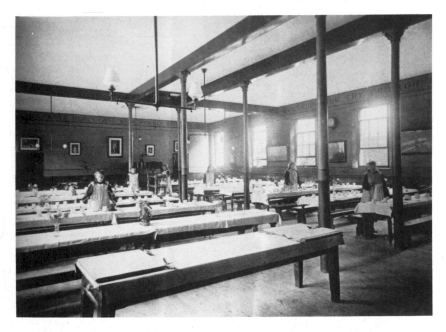

48 Once public concern for less-privileged children had risen in popularity, great pains were taken to ensure children's comfort. Note the religious verses at the top of the walls around this room in Derby, 1914.

49 Leeds, *c.*1901. This is one of a set of photographs taken to illustrate the appalling conditions in part of the city. This area was shortly to be cleared and these children, hopefully, given a better standard of life.

50 A cricket game in progress on the recreation field of a Derbyshire orphanage just after the outbreak of the Great War. The fielders appear to be more posed for the camera than the batsman. The opening of such institutions provided a much needed care for many children.

51 By late Edwardian times both public and Government concern for the physical well-being of less fortunate children were on the increase. This orphanage bathroom, stark by today's standards, would have indeed been a luxury to many children.

52 Anyone for tennis?

53 . . . and his hair fell down in ringlets.

54 The Victorian era was one of great scientific invention. Many inventions, particularly those connected with the railways, were miniaturised and sold as toys. This Staffordshire boy, from an affluent home, displays the latest equipment.

55 A well dressed group of children collecting summer flowers from Elland Woods in 1900.

56 Though beautifully dressed, skipping would have been most difficult. Nechells, Birmingham, c.1890.

57 Many children of the period were dressed in second hand and passed down clothes but this was better than the rags of others.

58 Runny-nosed, no taller than a brolly and gloriously happy in 1901.

59 My coat may be too big but it keeps me warm. *c.*1900.

60 Boy or girl? Birmingham, *c.*1890.

61 Haworth, home of the Bronte sisters, today receives thousands of visitors each year. The cobbled main street even looks much the same but the costumes of the local children have changed noticeably from this late nineteenth-century photograph. Is the child in the middle right really wearing a nightdress?

62 Bubbling with enthusiasm and showing no concern for their environment these two Yorkshire boys shared a joke either at or with the photographer.

63 Then as now cricket was a favourite pastime. These Derbyshire boys of the late Edwardian period had more time for pleasure pastimes than their early Victorian contemporaries.

64 *(Opposite)* Though many studio photographs were over-posed, nothing could detract from the beauty of these two Oxfordshire girls.

65 Children with a hot-pea seller in Westgate, Keighley about the 1890s. Of one such street trader it was said that he used to stir his peas with his wooden leg!

66 Posed photographs of children were not at all unusual. The situation, however, was often far better than this Leeds yard.

67 For many early amateur photographers, children provided the perfect subject. This little girl with her bar of chocolate posed for her grandfather. *c.*1905.

68 Nelson Boy Scouts are featured in this photograph of a postcard posted on
3 August 1910. The Scouts appear to be enjoying a mock battle and the photographer
no doubt encouraged by the skills developed during the Boer War in staging such
scenes, is using the Scouts to his best advantage.

70 By way almost of contrast, but taken about the same date, this family is obviously less well off. Nevertheless the children are well fed and obviously happy.

69 *(Opposite)* In the last decade of the 19th century family photographs had taken on a far more familiar look than the earlier stiffly posed studio photographs. This family photographed in 1893 were residents of Tong near Bradford. Particularly captivating are the near-identical dresses of the three girls and the son has made a decided effort to make his clothes look much as his father's.

71 Back-to-back houses meant there were no gardens and the children in this court had to make do with the paved area and cobbled streets. Nevertheless many entertaining games were found.

72 Unlike many of his contemporaries, this boy of the Edwardian period appears proud of his velvet and lace tunic. In evidence is the essential aspidistra which, usually in its blue bowl, followed a family from house to house, or simply grew and grew.

73 This photograph from a family album features a delightful nursery horse and cart. The child in the centre is wearing one of the popular sailor suits of the period. Note also the beautiful detail of the album surrounding the photograph.

74 A larger family group in Wolverhampton, 1880.

76 Some of the clothes worn by children before the turn of the century were hardly suitable for playing in. Contrast the clothes worn by this child to those in the street scenes. *c.*1890.

75 *(Opposite)* This photograph, taken in Leeds in 1901, well illustrates the conditions prevailing in many of our cities at the dawning of the new century. Photographs such as this could have been taken in almost any city and reflect that even though much change had taken place, very many children still lived in appalling conditions and were poorly dressed.

77 A pretty girl and spring flowers. *c.*1905.

4 Special occasions

78 Studio posed photographs were first popularised as cabinet photographs but later the more popular-sized 'carte de visite' was a great growth industry in the later years of Victoria's reign. Some parents went to extreme, even ridiculous lengths to show the qualities of their child.

81 Burnley Lads Club Band outside their Keighley Green premises before 1914. Most of these youths joined the 'Burnley Pals' of Captain Riley, the Club President.

79 & 80 These children about the turn of the century are taking part in a Pace-egg play. This form of Mummers play was widely performed in Lancashire and Yorkshire, usually at Easter time. The word 'pace' is a corruption of the Latin word 'pascha' meaning Easter.

82 Few children would have experienced the excitement of a ride on an early vehicle. Certainly the youngster on the back seat is enjoying himself while father and baby are not too happy. The vehicle was known as a 'locomobile' and could be seen in the early 1900s.

83 One of Burnley's most famous and earliest cars belonged to Sir James Mackenzie, the famous heart specialist, and was later bought by Mr E. Thompson (rear seat) with his son and daughter (front seat) 1904.

84 Concerts, often to raise money for charities, provided many children with entertainment. *c.*1907.

85 A concert held in a Derbyshire village school in 1912. The evening's entertainment was organised to raise money for a foreign missionary society. This photograph was taken, as were so many, by the proprietor of a local chemists' shop who had an interest in photography.

86 Two boys with prize winning guinea pigs about 1906. This photograph by Amos Dewhirst shows two brothers Herbert and Arthur Jerman. Arthur was to die of smallpox at Bosra during the Great War. For prize winners the boys look remarkably glum.

87 Mrs W.C. Anderson canvassing for the Keighley Parliamentary Bye-Election in October 1911. Mrs Anderson was the wife of the Labour candidate who in the event proved unsuccessful.

88 Electioneering seems somewhat lost on this little lad. October 1911.

91 *(Opposite)* Most photographs of the era were posed, some studio settings were so false as to be ridiculous.

89 An invitation card to local children from Lord Vernon of Sudbury Hall.

90 The Meynell Hunt outside Sudbury Hall. Note the tweed suited boy in the central foreground. *c.*1910.

92 It was pre-eminently a day for children. Over two thousand restless but happy children descended upon this Wisbech park and gratefully received small Union Jacks that the Coronation Committee provided. They joined a procession immediately behind the town band and formed its prettiest part. In the afternoon they returned to the park where the programme of events was mainly devoted to children's games and one girl was so lucky as to win 17/6d. 1902.

93 Beside a wall of advertisements the congregation of St Peter's Church, Burnley process to a Field Day 1907. Seemingly the smallest children led the way followed by the others in order of size. At one time Burnley was reputed to be one of the most heavily bill-posted towns in Lancashire.

94   Natural disasters always attract children's curiosity. The photograph was taken *c*.1912 at Northwich in Cheshire where subsidence from salt workings caused the collapse of this building. The gentleman leaning on his bicycle seems totally unconcerned.

95   Stockport Sunday Schools' 'Procession of Witness'. The sun was shining but thick dresses and suits, long stockings and boots were *de rigueur*.

96 Though not the ideal clothes for playing in they do show that this young boy should not have a difficult life ahead of him.

97 Heaton Lane, Stockport, Coronation Day, 1902. The children behind the band have obviously become bored with celebrating even though the Mayor has just passed.

8 St Thomas', Stockport, bonfire in celebration f Queen Victoria's Diamond Jubilee. The fire was med to be lit at 9.45pm 22 June 1897.

(Overleaf) It was not the dignitaries but ivering boys who took the first plunge into the ke at the opening of Roundhay Park, Leeds on 29 ine 1907.

100 A Sunday School or Chapel 'charity' or open air anniversary about 1900. Almost certainly Lancashire or Yorkshire.

101 The start of a Garland Day procession in Ayscoughfee Gardens, Spalding, Lincolnshire. Judging by the umbrellas this day was inclement. Garland Day was celebrated in many rural areas.

102   Whaley Bridge, Derbyshire, 28 July 1896, Sunday School outing. The children and teachers clad in their 'Sunday Best' which, of course, meant an obligatory hat. Many Victorian children had a staunch religious upbringing. Note particularly the bodice of the lady on far right. The lad lurking in the background reflects a sharp contrast in quality of clothing.

103   Rehearsing the Maypole Dance, Rectory Fields, Church Gate, Stockport 1901. The event was a Grand Maypole performance by 64 children on 23, 24, 25 and 26 October, in aid of the Tabernacle Sunday School Fund. The target was to raise £100 and Mr C.B. Fidler was the conductor. The Maypole dancing was part of a Grand Scenic Bazaar entitled 'Naples'.

104 A parade through the streets of Reddish, near Stockport by Houldsworth School pupils in 1912. The occasion appears to have been a rose fete, though whether the posies the children carried were all roses is not known.

105 As part of their Coronation procession the pupils of the Long Lee Wesleyan School, Keighley presented this historical tableaux 'Edward II and Queen Isabella'. The children in the foreground seem more interested in the camera than the procession.

106 1902 Coronation celebration for Edward VII in North Street, Keighley, W. Yorks. All over the county groups of children like these lined town and village streets. The small children being held in the upper left hand window seem in a rather precarious position.

107 A fair on Waterloo on Middle Hillgate, Stockport. Photographed 1894 by Mr T. Gould presumably because his son is the boy shielding his face in the near foreground.

108 Country picnics were a pleasant way of spending an afternoon. This photograph taken about 1890 shows a pram typical of the period.

109 Easter *c.*1905. Pendle Hills, Lancashire. The climbing of the renowned Pendle Hill was a traditional feature of Lancashire life around the turn of the century. Good Friday was the customary day for the start of the climbing season and young and old alike set out in great numbers. Children were told to take a stone to the top of the hill and pile it on the cairn to make the hill bigger but not to roll stones down as this could cause accidents. It is recorded that on one occasion a stone was rolled inflicting injury on another child climber, causing him to be carried away by stretcher.

110 Children and water are an inseparable combination. River Medina, Isle of Wight 1905.

111   Sports Days always have their prizes and prizegivers. On this occasion in 1908, books and shields appear to be the order of the day. The weather also looks to have co-operated.

5 At work

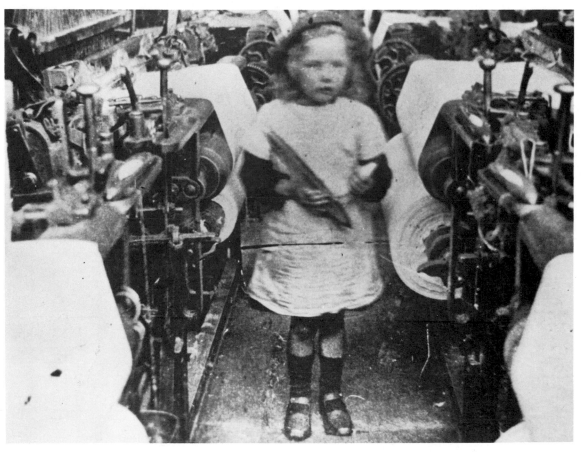

112   A little girl helps her mother in the mill by filling her shuttle for her. Small children were given many dangerous jobs in the mills resulting in often serious injury.

113   Child and adult workers mix together for this 1898 photograph. One of the interesting facets is the wide variety of dress styles.

114 On leaving school many children in Lancashire and Yorkshire became involved, like their parents, in the textile industry.

115 Working in such conditions as this was harmful to a person's health and thousands of people, including children, suffered chest complaints as a result.

116 A line of machines and a line of boys.

117 Children at work with their parents at a woad farm, Algairk, Lincolnshire. *c.*1900.

118 Wells Beach, Norfolk, *c.*1905. These bare-footed children wait hopefully for a chance to earn a few pence.

119 Workers from a spinning mill on 19 March 1896. Of particular interest in this photograph are the clogs worn by the children in the foreground. These children were probably half-timers although some of the older children no doubt worked full time. Note also the ornate gas lamp holder on the mill wall.

120 *(Overleaf)* Bill posters became a feature of many towns, amidst a collection of these a Halifax paper boy and baker's boy pause for a chat. 1910.

121 Cheerful children leaving a Yorkshire mill in 1902 alongside adults who do not have as much to smile about.

122 A street scene in Halifax *c*.1900. Before the day of the 'daily pinta' a boy makes his living selling milk from the churn. Photograph was taken at 10.35am.

123 Children have always worked with their parents on the land. These workers, mainly itinerant, were working on the Cambridgeshire Fens early this century. Note the Army Padre in the centre.

124 Children and parents worked side by side in the preparation of reeds for thatching. This photograph was taken on the Fenland marshes near Spalding, Lincolnshire. Even today at harvest time the family spirit still continues. *c*.1890.

125   Assembled in the Atlas Works yard, towards the end of the last century, the photograph shows the type of work open to many girls.

126 Although an obviously posed photograph this young boy, presumably an apprentice, appears happy at his work.

6 Holidays

127 Today's bathing beauties admired by tomorrow's. Railways opened up the seaside for day trips and the advent of the bathing machine meant that propriety could be preserved and a dip in the sea enjoyed. The young girls on the left make do with holding their skirts above their knees.

129 The visit of a travelling fair was a great occasion. In Northern mill towns the annual 'wakes' holidays provided the occasion for the visit of a fair. Children and adults alike would spend hours gazing at and listening to the sights and sounds.

128 *(Previous page)* High days and holidays in an Edwardian English summer, the period of relaxation before the Great War that was to follow.

130 The visit of a circus to Cromer about 1905. In addition to the organised show, the animals provided free entertainment, such as when the elephants went for a bathe in the sea. On these occasions a group of children from all walks of life was usually found close by.

131 By early Edwardian times the seaside holiday had become popular with a large number of families. Those who could not afford a week's holiday were able to make a day trip by train or charabanc. Holidays from work were, of course, unpaid so the day trip was the most popular. In this photograph of Southport, bucket and spade and donkey riding were an essential part of the day's visit.

133 *(Overleaf)* At many seaside towns local fishermen took advantage of the increase in visitors during the late Victorian and Edwardian period. The hiring out of beach chairs and bathing machines formed part of their business, as did the use of goat-drawn carts to provide rides on the beach. Often these carts were supervised by the fishermen's children. Cromer, *c.*1890.

132 Although built to carry mainly cargo, canal boats were also pressed into service to provide transport for day trips. Many Sunday School outings were held on the canal. Even the unromantic surroundings of a Yorkshire Gas Works did not dampen the enthusiasm.

134 School pupils on an outing to Morecambe on 6 October 1906. The photographer labelled his snapshot 'Chucking stones'.

135   A day by the river to paddle, climb rocks or simply watch was a great treat for many children. The rapid expansion of a railway network had made many places more readily accessible.

136   Taken on a north Norfolk Coast in 1905 a young girl, shoes over her shoulder, watches the traditional fishing boats return home. She seems somewhat incongruously dressed for paddling.

137 The pier, which during the period of this book became almost the symbol of a thriving holiday resort, here makes an excellent background for this group of children. The scene is thought to be one of the Lancashire resorts, probably Blackpool.